Portrait of Poulton-le-Fylde

Christine Storey

2007
Landy Publishing

ISBN 978-1-872895-73-4

A catalogue record of this book is available from the British Library.

Layout by Sue Clarke
Printed by Nayler the Printer Ltd., Accrington. Tel: 01254 234247

Landy Publishing have also published:

The Lancaster Canal in Focus by Janet Rigby
Life on the Lancaster Canal by Janet Rigby
Lancashire's Medieval Monasteries by Brian Marshall
Northward by Anthony Hewitson **
Bolland Forest & the Hodder Valley by Greenwood & Bolton **
A History of Pilling by F. Sobee **
Preston in Focus by Stephen Sartin
Glimpses of Glasson Dock by Ruth Z. Roskell
A Preston Mixture edited by Bob Dobson **

(Those marked ** are available at a reduced price when ordered direct from the publisher)

A full list of available publications is available from:

Landy Publishing
'Acorns' 3 Staining Rise, Staining, Blackpool, FY3 0BU
Tel/Fax: 01253 895678 (24hrs)
Email: peggie@peggiedobson.wanadoo.co.uk

INTRODUCTION

Some years ago I began researching my family history and was delighted to find my ancestors had lived in Poulton since around 1650, coming over the river Wyre from Hambleton and Out Rawcliffe. Once in Poulton they worked as flax dressers, bakers and joiners - their names appear in the records of the building of the Methodist Chapel - and also as landlords of the Plough and the Bay Horse.

Having one's roots in a place gives an added impetus and thrill to research and it is a pleasure to be able to share this interest with those who may read this book; I hope they find it enjoyable and interesting.

As a founder member of Poulton-le-Fylde Historical and Civic Society in 1981 I have been privileged to have access to the Society's archives, a collection of material made possible by the generosity of people who have loaned their precious photographs to be copied for the enjoyment of others.

I should like to thank several people whose help has much appreciated during the preparation of this book, in particular Mrs Gina Benson, Mrs Lisa Eland, Mrs Olive Highton, Mrs Cynthia Lee, Mr Eddie Pearce, Mrs Vera Pilkington, Mr Norman Short, Mr Tom Latto and Miss Audrey Waterman.

And special thanks to my husband Alan for his patience!

Christine Storey

POULTON

A photograph taken sometime in the 1880s. The cobbled Market Place in the centre of the town is wide, and at the far end on higher ground stands the parish church of St Chad.

On the right are two shops; Parkinson's saddlers and Lawrenson's general store. The imposing three-storey four-bay property next to them was the town house of the Walmsley family, later the police station and now the Masonic Hall and next to it a pair of single-storey cottages. At the far end is a three-storey property which served as a private house, a Cyclists' Rest and lastly as a bank.

Poulton, near Blackpool
E. C.—B.

At the corner of this building the Market Pace becomes Church Street, where the entrance to the Teanlowe Centre now is. In Church Street can be seen a row of whitewashed cobble-built cottages which included the Bay Horse and the Plough inns.

On the left can be seen the apex of the King's Arms, the first meeting place in Poulton of a group of Methodists.

The long stretch of property adjoining the pub was built as a unit during the 1730s as a result of a fire in 1732. Money to help pay for the rebuilding was collected nationally which took several years.

On the extreme left is what Poulton remembers as *'Richards'* an old fashioned ironmongers run during the 1870s and 1880s by Thomas Worthington.

The market cross, fish slab and whipping post are a remarkable set of items in town centre. The fact that there is no lamp – a purchase made with money left over from the collection made to celebrate Queen Victoria's golden jubilee in 1887 gives some indication of the photograph's date.

A photograph taken sometime after 1910 shows a large group of around seventy boys and girls – maybe a Sunday School trip? These were very popular: in 1875 the first Sunday School day trip to Lytham took place and so many went it was said Poulton was emptied.

The Market Place was a working space filled with livestock on market days. Market day was Monday and fairs for the sale of *cattle, cloth and peddlery* were held in February, April and November. By the 1920s the cattle market was also held on Saturdays. People were obviously intrigued by the camera.

For centuries Poulton has served as a commercial centre for the many small farms in the area. The Auction Mart was opened in 1897 behind the Golden Ball and for generations of school children it offered an exciting attraction during the school holidays. The complex included a calf ring, sheep pens and offices. A building with large double doors allowed bulls to be unloaded with safety; next to it was the bull ring. The shippon had stalls for 40 cows and a storage loft for hay and straw. A slaughterhouse stood near the railway and functioned until the start of the Second World War.

By the 1960s the need for an auction mart in the town was gone and it closed in 1969. The last of these buildings was demolished in 2006.

The stock pens and the sales in progress. Mr Bennett, a Poulton butcher, is on the left with Tracey Heywood the auctioneer.

COOKED
CHICKENS
A
SPECIALITY

George Edward Eyre

MEAT MANUFACTURER
(Group 1)

BURLINGTON AVENUE, POULTON-LE-FYLDE
Telephone: POULTON-LE-FYLDE 74 & 259.   Nr. BLACKPOOL

There were three abattoirs in Poulton; this one was at the end of Burlington Avenue, now the site of the Teanlowe Centre.

Two photographs taken from the top of the church tower overlooking the Golden Ball.
William Gaulter was the landlord between 1850 and 1864 when this was taken. The Preston and Wyre Railway station was still at the bottom of The Breck and the land behind this coaching inn was allotments and fields. The later, 1950s, picture shows the auction mart buildings, the railway line and the property on Lockwood Avenue.

Until the 1950s, Poulton and the neighbouring townships of Carleton and Hardhorn were surrounded by farms; Greenbank Farm was in Argyle Road and is now the site of apartments named *'Greenbank'*.

Looking towards the parish church from the present Queensway, this land was used for stock awaiting slaughter in the abattoir – the building with the short upper roof to the right of the picture.

Little Poulton, as its name denotes, was a small hamlet on the edge of the town. This photograph shows one of the small farms, built, as was the custom, side on to the road with a small orchard in front. This property was replaced by modern housing.

Vicarage Road once led straight through to Little Poulton – the path can be traced on older maps and the route can still be walked. Apart from Little Poulton Hall, there were eight or nine households, mainly farmers and agricultural labourers.

11

The top photograph shows Poulton's tithe barn in the 1960s.

Ben Edwards, the former Lancashire County Archaeologist, and officers from Wyre Borough Council examine the Tithebarn. Although there was support for its preservation, it was demolished in 1969. The site is now a car park. During the 19th century it had been used as a theatre for travelling companies of actors, and at the end of its time, housed many small workshops including a tinsmith.

Poulton tithe barn occupied a site very close to St Chad's church fronting on to one of the six main roads leading off the Market Place. The siting of the tithe barn so close to the church, in a street named Tithebarn Street, suggests it was ancient although no date was ever attributed to it. Tithes have been collected by the parish from the 9th century. It was required that every parishoner gave one tenth of his produce in kind to the parish priest for the maintenance of clergy, the church and all the business of the parish. By the 19th century there were objections both from religious dissenters and from farmers who were bearing the load which was not shared by manufacturers in the cities. Poulton tithes were commuted to rents in 1849.

During the bathing season visitors would come to Poulton from Blackpool and would be entertained by performances in the tithe barn which by 1822 was in use as a theatre, at a time before there were any in Blackpool. At other times of the year the tithe barn was used for threshing with flails.

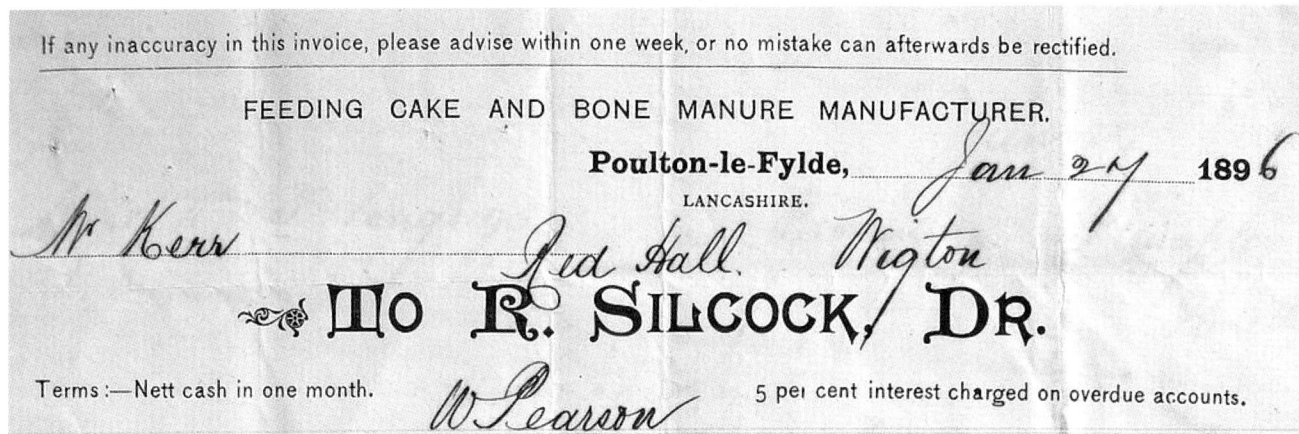

An 1896 bill from local provender merchant Silcock's. The name became familiar as *'Silcock's Corner'*, on Lambs Road, Thornton. W Pearson, whose order included specialist meal and cake for rearing and fattening livestock, was a farmer in Wigton, Cumbria

An unusual view of St Chad's church; missing are the large palm trees planted along the south side.

Jack Whalley on his way home from school in 1930. The basket in his right hand held the remains of his lunch which he had taken to school that day, as had all the school children

Until 1973 the churchyard was a mass of gravestones. Although most dated from the mid 19th century, the churchyard has been used for over a thousand years. The older stones have not survived. It was closed to burials in 1881 when Moorland Road cemetery was opened by the newly formed Poulton Burial Board. Old churches always have a hostelry close to one of the gates and here we see the Thatched House. St Chad's parish stretched from what is now Squires Gate Lane, Blackpool to Singleton. After a long walk or horse ride to attend the parish church services on Sundays, refreshments would be welcome. The large pointed stone on the right is a memorial to a teetotaller

The altar in St Chad's originally stood against the east wall, but in 1868 an apse was added to the east wall, paid for by the vicar the Rev. Thomas Clarke. Some graves had to be removed from in front of the east wall where the apse was to be built. These included that of Edward Sherdley with its *'skull and crossbones'* – the popular emblem of death. This stone now lies at the bottom of the steps leading to the vestry.

A local myth says this is a pirate's grave and local children love to run round it three times to raise his ghost. They are often surprised to find the person they raise instead is the vicar coming out of the vestry door.

The Rev Jim Stretch was the vicar at St Chad's for 19 years and died in 1973. He was the first British forces chaplain to enter Belsen were he helped to bury thousands in mass graves. A newsreel photographer who had been with Jim Stretch later wrote *'He worked like ten men; distributing clothing, helping feed the sick, giving comfort and holding services with his colleagues'*.

The Wesleyan Methodist Chapel. The first Wesleyan chapel was built in 1819 on the corner of Queen's Square and Chapel Street. Although numbers were still small, the chapel was enlarged in 1861 and a Sunday School was opened, with about 45 children attending.

A wedding takes place at the Methodist church in the 1930s. A dry cleaners which now stands on the site of the chapel carries the notice *Cleanliness is next to Godliness* – an appropriate comment!

An increase in the population of Poulton between 1880 and 1890 led the trustees to plan a new chapel to the north of the existing one with the original building accommodating the Sunday School. The photograph shows stonelaying for these extensions in 1892.

Cllr R. P. Tomlinson took a keen interest in Wesleyanism and preached from local pulpits, becoming one of the best known non-conformist preachers in the land, travelling from Lands End to John O'Groats and becoming Vice President of the Methodist Conference

The foundation stone for the new Methodist church in Queensway was laid on March 7th 1964 and the new building was opened on New Year's Day 1965. Poulton's maritime tradition provided the inspiration for the design

The Independent Chapel stands on the corner of Queensway and Tithebarn Street.

A *'small commodious Independent chapel'* was built at a cost of about £450 and opened on April 11th 1809 on a road at that time called Longfield Lane. Over the years the chapel was to be closed for periods of time and was at one time used as a warehouse.

In 1886 the chapel was re roofed and re-seated for 195, making it *'one of those comfortable little country chapels of which the denomination need not be ashamed'*. By the end of the century membership of the church had increased so that a new building was erected. Built of red brick and completed in 1899, it replaced the old chapel which was to be used as the Sunday School.

The land for the new church was given by Robert Bainbridge's family, whose home, *'Chatsworth House'*, stood close by on Longfield Lane, the original name for the west end of Tithebarn Street. In October 1973 the Congregational Church merged with the Presbyterians to form the United Reformed Church. The building was redesigned in 2007 to be used once again as a chapel.

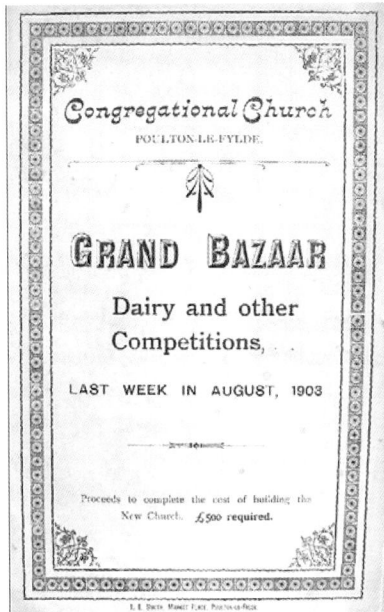

Congregational Church
POULTON-LE-FYLDE.

GRAND BAZAAR

Dairy and other
Competitions,

LAST WEEK IN AUGUST, 1903

Proceeds to complete the cost of building the
New Church. £500 required.

Final fund raising for the costs of the new church continued into 1903. Described as a '*neat Gothic edifice*' it seated 400 and cost £2,700 to build.

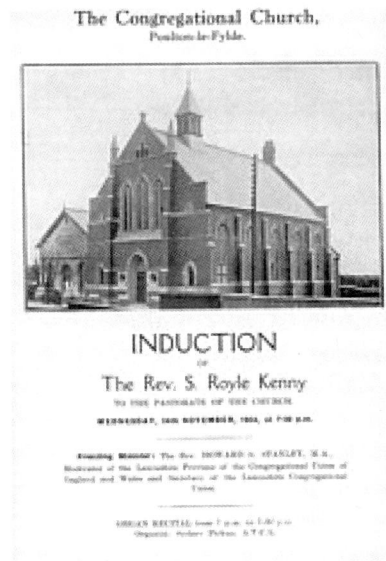

A programme for the induction of the Rev S Royle Kenny in 1954.

The Congregational Church,
Poulton-le-Fylde.

INDUCTION
OF
The Rev. S. Royle Kenny

Church Street, one of the main thoroughfares leading off the Market Place, housed two pubs – the Bay Horse on the extreme left and the Plough - its position indicated by the lamp extended from the wall on the left. A third pub - the Golden Ball - is in the distance. The four-storey building on the right was one of three lodging houses in Poulton. Known as *'Twenty Steps'*, here stayed itinerant workers, mainly from Ireland, who came to Poulton for work at harvest time. The surrounding farms relied entirely on this extra help with the harvest and money earned was taken back to the workers' families at the end of the hiring. The notice painted onto the property on the right was a permanent advert for the Palace Theatre Blackpool.

Poppy sellers in the Market Place in November 1921. The first official British Legion Poppy Day was held in Britain on 11 November 1921, inspired by the poem *'In Flanders' Fields'* by John McCrae. Since then the Poppy Appeal has been a key annual event in the nation's calendar.

There is much of interest in Poulton Market Place. This photograph shows a walkabout around the town centre led by Jim Firth of Poulton Historical Society in the 1980s.

The war memorial was placed here in 1921, the year of the first British Legion poppy appeal. When it was moved to its present position in the market place it had to be split into seven sections and loaded onto a truck by crane and sling. The memorial was, and is now, surrounded by small white pebbles. They were originally laid by families of service men who lost their lives in the war and each pebble represents a dead serviceman. As part of the re-ordering of the Square in the 1970s, old sett stones were brought in from Morecambe to retain the link with the old roads in the town.

In 1837 two deputy constables were put on duty on Saturday and Sunday evenings for a fortnight as an experiment. It was obviously a success. The document shows a list of twelve Special Constables drawn up in July 1837. In 1839, Giles Thornber proposed to the vestry meeting that there should be a town lockup *for the good and safety of the town'*. In 1842 legislation concerning the appointment and payment of parish constables was introduced and a list of twenty men nominated to be constables in Poulton was sent to the magistrates who controlled their appointment. These were in addition to the newly-formed paid constabulary.

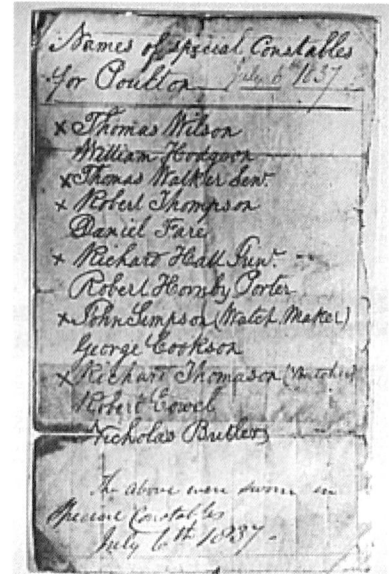

The first purpose built police station was built at a cost of £3,500 and opened in 1895. It was a single-storey building with the main entrance in the tunnel at the side. In the yard at the rear were two police houses and the station provided accommodation for one sergeant, a constable and a weights and measures officer. The last of the houses was occupied by a police sergeant up to the 1960s. An upper floor was added to the station in 1960.

The station originally had three cells and a charge office where prisoners were taken before being locked up. After extensive alterations over the years this one remaining cell has been retained in its original condition.

A sergeant and four constables in the police station yard in 1908.

In 1989 four officers re-enacted the photograph: Sergeant Bob Dobson and PCs Tony Thornburrow, Frank Horsfall and Ron Garner.

The next four photographs show the building development which took place on the east side of the Market Place between the 1870s and 1900. The transformation sees the old four-storey home of the Walmsley family become the Masonic Hall re-fronted in brick. The two-storey cottages and the three-storey house next to them are replaced by an imposing pseudo-Tudor block which in very short time is itself replaced by the single-storey police building which is part of the present police station

In the 1840s the majority of the properties on both sides of the Market Place were houses and shops, and those on the west side remained remarkably stable up to the present day. In the 19th century the shop next to the King's Arms was a watchmaker's for 40 years, next but two was a hairdresser's which for many years doubled as the post office. This was the period when drapers' shops proliferated, with one on this side run by Thomas Smith's family who printed Thornber's *History of Blackpool* in 1837. As early as 1841 the property was listed as a bookseller.

On the east side was Braithwaite Bond, grandfather of William Hodgson and later to be the town's auctioneer. In the 1840s he was a boot and shoe maker. In amongst the mix of houses and shops were a grocer, a druggist, and an ironmonger. In 1851 there appears to have been a school on this side run by Elizabeth Rogers, the daughter of Hannah Rogers - proprietor of houses - with 8 pupils living there. The two shops on the right were Parkinson's, a saddler and Lawrenson's. Thomas Lawrenson had run this general dealers since the mid 1860s. Many older inhabitants remember his daughter Maggie Lawrenson who ran the business as a newsagents. His son William Lawrenson became a great collector of items about the local history of Poulton and served as the verger at St Chad's.

The property at the far end of the photographs was a house with two frontages, one facing the Market Place and the other Church Street. Apart from the introduction of two shops, it retained the same appearance throughout this time, at one point becoming a Cyclists' Rest as the popularity of cycling developed in the area. Some time after 1910 it was re-faced and became a bank. It was demolished in 1938.

Licensed Dealer in Game.

D. E. Lawson
Fishmonger
and
Poulterer
English & Foreign Fruiterer
Breck Street,
~ **Poulton-le-Fylde**

All Orders Promptly Attended to and Delivered
TELEPHONE No. 20

J. T. SWARBRICK
BOOT & SHOE
MAKER
CHURCH STREET, POULTON-LE-FYLDE.
REPAIRS
ON THE SHORTEST NOTICE.
Hand-Sewn Boots
MADE TO ORDER.
All Orders receive prompt attention.

NOTE ADDRESS—
CHURCH STREET

27

Richards' ironmongers was well known to many generations of Poulton people.

The foundations of the business were laid by John Hodgson, an ironmonger and grocer in 1754. Over the following years it had several owners, till 1847 when Robert Dunderdale took it over. He developed the nail trade, sending nails to Barrow and the surrounding districts. In 1874, Thomas Worthington was running the business which he extended, adding a warehouse and trading as a baker and dealer in flour. By 1891, John Roe had taken it on. He let the grocery business slide in favour of ironmongery, making his own tin-ware such as milking cans and milk kits. He developed the oil and paint trade and the sale of agricultural implements and took a great interest in bee keeping and the production of honey. In 1895 Ebenezer Richards from Bolton, took over and took on adjoining premises.

Here is Bill Richards. When the business finally closed in 1979 traces of the 18th century building could still be seen in the shop - a stone-flagged floor, solid rough hewn beams in the ceiling and walls three feet thick.

In 1909 D. T. Brown left his home in Perth and travelled by train to the Fylde where he set up a wholesale seed business in Poulton as a seed and bulb merchant in Bull Street. Although business mainly was with growers for the food market, Browns also made their seed catalogues available to amateur gardeners.

Browns Seed Merchants moved to new buildings in Station Road in 1927, when this photograph was taken. The firm is now based at Newmarket in Suffolk

ESTABLISHED 1892

MAYOR & SONS

Pork Butchers

TRY OUR NOTED PORK PIES, SAUSAGES, AND COOKED MEATS.

POULTON-LE-FYLDE

Mayor's butchers was set up by James Mayor in 1892. He was born in Preston and his father George, who was born in Woodplumpton, had a variety of jobs, including railway porter and landlord of the Old Keys Head on Friargate, Preston. However James' mother Alice came from Stalmine, and, after his father's death, James and his wife moved with his mother to Hudson's Farm in Out Rawcliffe. From there he set up in business in Poulton as a pork butcher

and made his home in Holly Street, now called Hayfield Avenue, off Station Road. In 1994 when the roof of Mayor's shop - shown in the photograph with a canopy above the window - was being repaired, old wood was found in the roof timbers with marks of scorching, re-used after the fire of 1732. James died in 1912 and Mary took on the business. She died in 1930 and their son George Herbert took over.

William Jones was a bookseller & printer in the Market Place - and also had a circulating library in the 1830s; in the photograph the shop has a white blind in the window. This is likely to have been the predecessor of Thomas Smith who printed Thornber's *'History of Blackpool'* in 1837.

In the early 1840s Margaret Smith, a widow with six young children, was running the shop -- and in time it developed so that by 1861 Margaret, now 70, was working with five of her adult children, all described as *'stationers and printers'*.

A fire in the shop in 1936 had a tragic sequel - the death of Tom Smith. A local newspaper reported *'Tom Smith was born in the very house in which he was found after the fire. He had lived in the same house all his life. His father, Tom, had also lived in the same house and conducted the same business - printer & stationer. He invariably had with him his gun and dog. Tom's grandfather - Tom - was a very famous scholar and at one time Headmaster of the Free Charity school from 1825 – 1831'.*

Windsor Woollies - Benjamin and Elizabeth Windsor were caretakers at Alkincoates Hall near Colne. Elizabeth was a clever, prize-winning needlewoman. She used a hand knitting machine to make her children's clothes which were much admired and led to their first shop being opened in Colne, the house behind the shop becoming the first Windsor factory. During World War One they made khaki pullovers for the services and at the end of the war shops across the country were placing orders for their knitted clothes. In 1923 a factory was purchased in Buchanan Street, Blackpool and in 1928 another factory was designed and built on Station Road Poulton. A factory was later built in Garstang. Production ceased in Poulton in 1992.

Benjamin Corless Sykes was a solicitor born in 1852. In 1895 he built a grand house named *'The Manor'*, on land just off Moorland Road. In the early 1900s he opened it to the general public with an exhibition of art and curios, offering afternoon teas and organising trips to The Manor from Cleveleys and Blackpool. An advert in *'The Blackpool, Lytham & Fleetwood Gazette'* reads: *To Blackpool visitors - New drive to the magnificent country mansion The Manor Poulton-le-Fylde, (off Moorland Road). Ornamental Gardens, and extensive collection of pictures and art treasures. Admission 6d Children 3d. Teas and other refreshments. Tuesdays and Thursday 1s. (Tea included). Closed on Sundays. The Manor is also within walking distance of Poulton Station'.* The building became a private house, a vegetarian guest house, the training school for Rediffusion and is now a nursing home.

Inside the walls and doors are covered in beautifully painted murals.

In 1834 letters arrived by horse post from Preston at 9am and left at 2pm to and from Blackpool by foot at 10 am & half past 1pm.

Poulton means *"farmstead by a pool or creek"*. 'The addition of *'le-Fylde'* was added to the name in 1842 when the penny post began, to stop local post mistakenly being sent north to the village of Poulton-le-Sands, now part of Morecambe.

In 1934 the post office moved from the square where it had been housed in the shop in James Baines' house to the Breck. The third move was to this site in Church Street. When the Teanlowe centre was opened in 1972 the post office moved to its present position.

Long's bookshop next to the post office was once the site of the Plough Inn and at the time of this photograph still had an old fireplace close to the shop window. The business is now a cooked meat shop.

This *'penny post'* stamp was issued to Poulton in 1838

Poulton·
PennyPost

With the opening of the Preston & Wyre Railway, the mail coach was replaced with a mail cart. Sir Peter Fleetwood Hesketh contributed £50 per year towards the running costs

Post boys relaxing outside the Post Office which was the shop on the ground floor of James Baines House, which can be seen in the background.

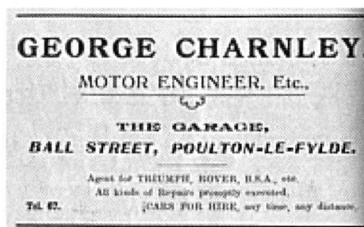

Born in Middlesex in 1830, Adolph Viener was a gold jeweller with premises in Talbot Road Blackpool. He died in 1892 and his wife Kate moved into the White House in Queen's Square with her two daughters Edith and Ethel.

The White House, an imposing three-storey property, still carries its name on the front wall and can be seen in the distance in this photograph. Ethel founded scouting in Poulton and Edith began the Third Poulton Guides at St Chad's. Edith also worked with the British Legion, founded the NSPCC in Poulton and was Superintendent of St Chad's Sunday School. Their brother Harry was to become a clergyman and left the family home when he moved to Walsall.

James Baines was born & grew up in Nether Wyresdale in the parish of Garstang and died in 1717 in Poulton. Baines' house still stands in the Market Place and he would have a good view from the front room windows of the stocks and whipping post where beggars of all ages would be punished, together with wrong-doers.

James left money for the free education of poor boys in three schools he had built in Poulton, Marton and Thornton with money for apprenticeships. The Baines Trust is still in existence as a charity and the three schools still benefit from their founder's original investment in land.

The Poulton school was re-built in 1828 using some of the material from the original building. The new school was paid for by public subscription and consisted of one room *'14 yards by 6 yards'*. In 1878 the school had to close through a shortage of pupils. In 1881 the old building was restored and the school re-opened the following year as an endowed school with 35 boys. In 1899 the name was changed to *'Baines Grammar School'*.

The *'School House'* in the photograph was built in 1892 as the head master's house. Next to it is the original single-storey school building.

Presentation of awards at a sports event at the school in the later 1890s.

The school prospectus shows a typical grammar school curriculum of the early 1920s.

Sir William Hodgson at the ceremony of laying the foundation stone for the new buildings in 1931. The stone itself appears to have been hidden by subsequent additional building work.

The Castle Gardens pub was once a dwelling house from which beer was bought and was known by the sign of the *'Hole in The Wall'*. It became known as the *'Weld Arms'* because until the 1860s much of the land in Carleton was owned by the Weld family of Lulworth Castle in Dorset. The *'Castle Garden Pleasure Gardens'* were opened at the Weld Arms in 1884 and over the years an aviary, a bowling green, tennis lawn, ornamental lake and swings were added. During the late 19th century, the Castle Gardens was developed as a centre for entertainment and attracted large numbers of people on holiday in Blackpool. Horse-drawn wagonettes brought visitors to the bowling greens, gardens, children's entertainments and menagerie.

Carleton is one of 63 communities in the Fylde listed in the Domesday Survey of 1086. The name derives from *'the farm of the peasants'*. In medieval times Carleton was much larger than now and until the 20th century stretched from Layton to Thornton and took in large parts of Bispham. It was divided into two main areas, with Norcross at its northern end bordering on Thornton; this was known as *'Great Carleton'* and stretched from Norcross to what is now High

Furlong, with the remaining area as far as Layton being known as *'Little Carleton'*. Carleton had consisted entirely of farms until the middle years of the 20th century when large scale building changed the face of the township. Many of the 35 small farms which existed in 1850 have disappeared under housing, but a few farm houses still remain as private houses and there are now at least two working farms.

Carleton school was set up as a result of the will of Elizabeth Wilson of Whiteholme who died in 1680 and left instructions for her money to be used to buy land and set up a school for poor children of Carleton. In 1839 another building was erected on the site. In 1902 a red brick building was erected next to the old one. The present school was built in 1969 when the old buildings were demolished to be replaced by housing.

Carleton Gala was held on a 2 acre field at the back of Carleton school. The gala procession began at the Curve Halt on Tithebarn Street, went to Rington Farm on Fleetwood Road then to Pye's Farm near the crematorium. Crowning took place at the Castle Gardens after a two hour, nearly three mile walk. Carleton was a farming community - the few properties which stood by the crossroads – then known as *'Four Lane Ends'* - were inhabited by tradesmen such as a rope maker, a butcher, a shoemaker and a wheelwright, and agricultural labourers.

In July 1970 a piece of spare land in High Furlong on the boundary between Poulton and Blackpool provided an archaeological find of international significance. As the earth was being prepared for house building, an almost complete skeleton of an elk was revealed. It was subsequently dated as around twelve thousand years old. Particular significance lay in the injuries to the bones and barbed tips which lay close by, one embedded in one of the animal's hind legs just above the hoof. The evidence of barbs in the animal's leg showed that the elk had been hunted and had drowned in what had then been a lake, surrounded by trees and shrubs. This chance discovery has proved to be the earliest evidence of man in the North West. At this time Britain was part of the mainland of Europe and the area which was to become Poulton lay far from the sea

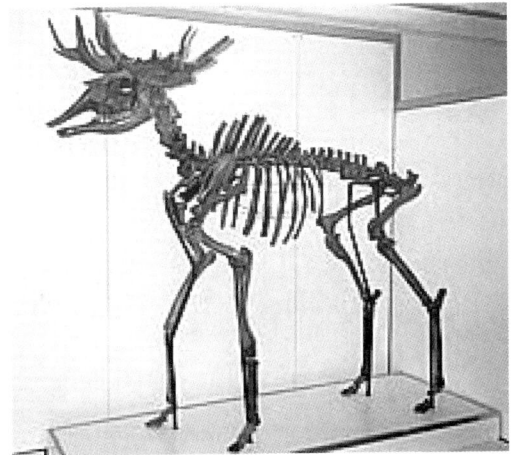

The photographs show the elk which is on show in the Harris Museum in Preston and the family who first found the remains examining the bones outside their house. Most people are surprised at the size of the elk which was the size of a shire horse.

The old station at the bottom of the Breck became used for goods traffic when the new station was opened. By the end of 2006 virtually nothing remained of the site.

The Royal Oak hotel still stands on the opposite corner of Station Road to the old station. Until the coming of the railway line this road was known as *'Back Street'*. This was a name frequently used, referring to a street which ran round the back of the town.

The *'Railway & Station Hotel'* stood on the Breck Road facing Station Road. Its chimneys can be seen in the top left hand corner of the photograph of the old station. The hotel also advertised *'posting, hearse and mourning coaches available'*.

This invoice dated September 1st 1903 refers to the executors of the late Miss Poole. It is for a hearse to Rawcliffe Cemetery, a funeral carriage, five single coaches at 15 shillings each and two drivers at two shillings each.

Work on the new station began in 1894. The old station at the bottom of the Breck was to become the goods station. Before building could begin, land and buildings had to be bought from about 40 owners near the route of the new railway line, and several properties in Tithebarn Street and on the Breck were demolished. The road had to be raised 9 feet to lead up to the bridge.

The tight curve on the line to Blackpool built in 1846 can be seen at the bottom left in this photograph. It was the cause of a fatal crash when a tripper train returning from Blackpool to Wigan was de-railed in 1892. At the inquest the driver was quoted as not being drunk as he had only had four pints of beer.

In March 1923 Poulton Curve station was built and remained in use until 29th November 1952. The railway house still stands on Tithebarn Street just by the railway bridge. During the 1990s, the whole area was turned into a park incorporating the disused railway line - now a haven for wildlife.

The Jubilee Arch was built by Mr H I Parry – often referred to as 'Judge Parry' - in 1897 to commemorate the diamond jubilee of Queen Victoria. Mr Parry shared the role of Blackpool Registrar with his son Wykeham and their family name is commemorated in Parry Way which leads off Breck Road into the Civic Centre. The Jubilee Arch stood at the entrance to his home 'Woodlands', number 46 Breck Road. This house was to become part of the Convalescent Home built by a partnership of the Cotton Operatives and mill owners. It was known as the 'Joseph Cross Memorial Home'. In the 1960s the property was turned into a training college for teachers.

A farm and farm buildings adjoined the college and these, together with the arch, were replaced by a community building known appropriately as 'The Shippon'

This window commemorated Joseph Cross, the union official after whom the Convalescent Home was named. The Home was opened in 1931. He came from Blackburn and was remembered as a quiet man who rose to high office in his Trade Union

In October 1973 it was reported that plans for enlarging the college would double its size to over 1,000 students and would cost £570,000. But these plans were not followed up and, with a change of national policy, the college closed. In 1974, Woodlands became the Wyre Borough Council's Civic Centre.

The first record of Breck House is on a map drawn up in 1684 in which it is labelled *'Mr Pattison'*. In the early 19th century it was owned by William Catterall together with 24 acres of land in the area which he farmed. The property passed to members of the Sykes family and by 1938 it had become a convalescent home named *'Seafield'*.

During the 1930s Mary Macarthur Convalescent Homes were set up for *'the relief of women in need by the provision of holidays for such persons in need by reason of age, poverty, infirmity, disablement or social or economic circumstances.'* In early 1950s Breck House became part of the Mary Macarthur Trust.

Mary Macarthur was born in Glasgow in 1880. She was converted to the cause of trade unions by a speech made by John Turner about how badly some workers were being treated by their employers. In 1903 Mary moved to London where she became Secretary of the Women's Trade Union League. She died in 1921.

In the late 19th century Breck House had been the home of Benjamin Sykes, a great exhibitor of horses. When the property was demolished for new housing in the early 21st century the brick arch which had stood in front of the house was removed across the road to stand near to St John's Catholic Church.

Breck Road

On the left of the photograph is the turning into Moorland Road and the burial ground of the Catholic church of St John the Evangelist. The white building is Breck Lodge, now a nursing home, one of Poulton's oldest remaining houses.

On the right in the distance is the '*Railway Hotel*' built around 1839 and later named the '*Railway and Station Hotel*'. Beyond it a house with a barn and stableyard, demolished to make way for extensions to Poulton Training College in the 1960s.

The original church of St John the Evangelist stood at the bottom of the Breck, at the end of a tree-lined drive, surrounded by fields. It was built, as was the custom at the end of the 18th Century, away from the main road, unobtrusive and secluded; a simple rectangular building incorporating both chapel and priest's house, without visible decoration or embellishment.

In the early years of the 20th century, the original chapel building was closed and a new church built close by. In 1983 the old church became a Grade II listed building.   It is now used as the church hall.

Hardhorn Road leading towards Poulton, the bend in the road shows it is a view from just south of where the Garstang Road traffic lights would stand when the road was built in the 1930s.

Golf was played at Poulton Links off the Breck, close to the site of the current course. It provided a round of social and competitive events throughout the summer.

Built in the early 1894/5 of Accrington brick, these substantial properties are on Highcross Road. Round the bend in the road to the right, is the junction with Hardhorn Road.

JENKINSON'S CORNER SHOP,
The Breck, Poulton-le-Fylde

JUST MAKE A NOTE OF THE ABOVE ADDRESS,

AND IF YOU

REQUIRE

Newspapers and Periodicals Promptly Delivered,
Stationery, Post-Cards, Heraldic China.
School and Office Requisites, Pencils, Rubbers, &c.
The Latest Jokes, Tricks, Games, and Puzzles.
Music, Books, Paper Doyleys, Mats, and Pie Frills.

PLEASE CALL, AND YOU WILL NOT REGRET DOING SO.

JOHN KIRKHAM
PAINTER, DECORATOR & PAPER HANGER
CERTIFIED PLUMBER

Gas, Water, and
Electrical
Fittings.
Modern and
Up-to-date.

BRECK
STREET
POULTON-LE-FYLDE.

The Thatched House, one of Poulton's oldest buildings. When it was demolished in 1910 it was a *'cruck framed'* building with two tree trunks forming the basis for its walls. The present building which replaced it is much larger. In 1913 it advertised *'good accommodation for motorists and cyclists'*.

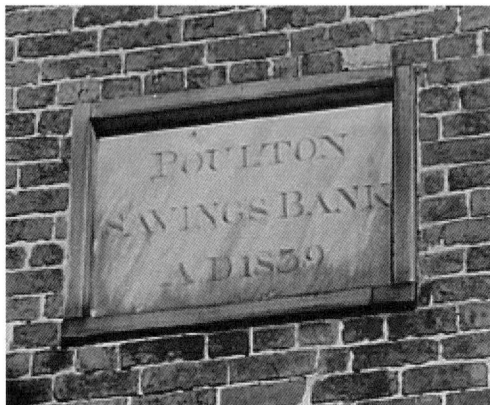

On the corner of Chapel Street and Vicarage Road stands a building with this date stone high on its front wall. It was built on ancient *'glebe'* land which had once belonged to the church and had a small cottage as part of its construction. The site of its front door can still be seen on the side of the building. It was used to house the town's lending library in the 1880s.

The old vicarage was replaced in the late 1950s. During the first War it served as a convalescent home for service men and many social events were held in its large grounds. A tennis court stood on the site until the late 1990s.

In the early nineteenth century many of the properties on the Breck – a name meaning *'a slope'* – were still private houses, some with workshops. Owners on the west side included Giles Thornber, John Ball, Richard Ball, William Gornall and Thomas Jolly. On the east corner with Ball Street was the Ship Inn, then a series of cottages one of which was a joiner's workshop; close to where the station now is was a smithy. This photograph looks down the Breck from Ball Street; it carried two-way traffic until a one way system was introduced in the 1980s.

By the middle of the century the Breck, then known as *'Breck Street'*, was beginning to show signs of developing into a shopping centre particularly the east side: the Ship still had the same landlord but next door was a fruiterer, a plasterer and slater, a joiner and builder, coal merchant and a coal dealer, a dressmaker and a milliner. On the opposite side the Pattisons, Jollys and Gornall and Thornbers remained in their private houses. The commercialisation of Breck Street continued so that virtually every household was providing a trade or service.

Foster's shop on the Breck is still in existence, although under another name.

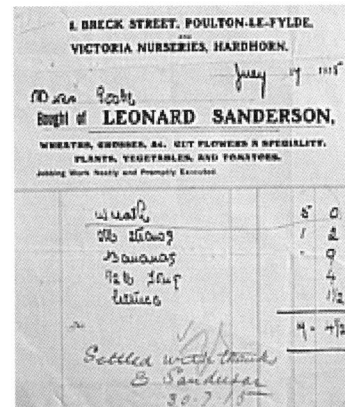

The King's Arms can be seen with its pointed roof line just to the left of the street lamp. It stood on the corner of Burlington Avenue, now the Royal Bank of Scotland, at the entrance to the Teanlowe Centre.

The Bay Horse in Church Street became the Town Hall after Poulton Urban District Council was set up in 1900. After local government reorganisation in 1974 a civic centre was opened at the bottom of the Breck and the town hall became a pub once again, renamed the Old Town Hall rather than taking its former name to prevent confusion with another pub named the Bay Horse in Thornton

The Queen's Hotel, Lower Green, was opened in 1901 and demolished in 2006 to be replaced by apartments.

A gala float outside the Ship Inn in 1913.

The Ship was popular with seamen from Fleetwood, navvies on construction work, local farmers and tradesmen. It was a headquarters for the trotting track men, their bookies and supporters. Trotting pony races took place in a stadium at Skippool. Fights took place in the back yard, for which betting was arranged, and possibly cock fights in the loft above the stables. The Ship became a Working Men's Club and later the Conservative Club. In 2000 it opened as '*The Cube*'.

This emblem of a sailing ship can be seen in the brickwork close to the roof, on two sides of the property. One faces onto Vicarage Road and the other onto the Breck.

This is Thomas Darville. At the turn of the 20th century, his wife Nancy had a grocer's shop in the Market Place while Thomas sold produce from his handcart round the streets of Poulton. The family typifies employment in the town; the eldest daughter helped in the shop, the next was a dressmaker, the son was an errand boy.

In the early years of the nineteenth century a house in Queen's Square was the home of Mr Harrison, owner of a business manufacturing sacking, sail cloth and sheeting. He employed thirty to forty people in weaving sheds situated behind the house. The property was later used as the workhouse for Poulton and small looms were installed to give employment to the poor who came there.

This fine building was once a coaching inn – the *Spread Eagle*. From the 1930s this grocer's shop was run by the Reeds, father and then son. By the 1980s, family run grocers such as this were a rarity - forty different spices sold by the ounce, loose tea and coffee beans waiting to be ground. Bill Reed ran a delivery service for customers outside Poulton. In pre-war days the staff would go round to the four or five big estates in Poulton to meet the cooks, discuss what foods were in season and write down the order for the week.

For the finest supplies of BEEF, MUTTON, VEAL and LAMB, try

J. COUPE, Family Butcher,

Tel. 195.
Residence 83.   **QUEEN'S SQUARE, POULTON-LE-FYLDE.**

Specialities also : Corned Beef, Pickled Tongues, Home-Cured Hams and Bacon.

In the mid 1850s, Robert Parkinson from Treales and his wife Mary settled in Poulton. Agnes, Robert's sister, married William Tomlinson from Thornton and they had three sons - Robert Parkinson Tomlinson, Thomas McNeal Tomlinson and John Maynard Tomlinson. Robert was a J.P. and Chairman of Poulton UDC six times between 1910 & 1937. In 1928 he became Liberal MP for Lancaster.

This shop was on the corner of Queen's Square and Chapel Street - the old Methodist church can be seen behind the coach. The Methodist Church once a year had a coach trip for a mothers and children's group. In 1936, cousins Lionel, aged three, and four year old Eric, were left in the driver's cab as the party prepared for the outing. The boys pretended to drive the coach and Lionel decided to move the big lever out of his way. As the driver jumped onto the step to unlock the door and open the coach for the passengers, it started to roll forward, gaining speed down the incline and ending up crashing into the corner shop leaving an orderly queue standing on the pavement watching in horror.

Hardhorn Road was once known as 'Sheaf Street' after the hostelry of that name which stood opposite the school. For generations the school was popularly known as 'Sheaf Street School' until it changed its name to St Chad's Church of England Primary School in 2000. The children experience a very different school life from their ancestors.

Sheaf Street schoolroom with Miss Elizabeth Tebay, the headmistress. Two sisters - Elizabeth and Anne Jane – taught at the school for many years. The family had moved to Fleetwood in the 1870s and in the early 1900s they moved to Moorland Avenue, Poulton. Two other sisters, Anne and Isabella, were teachers in St Annes. During Elizabeth's time as headmistress, the annual festival was planned and run from the school and she was responsible for the organisation. She died in 1920.

Poulton Gala started as a *'club day'* in 1795. In 1897 *'Club Day'* became known as *'Poulton Children's Festival'*, when, for the first time, the children took an active part in it and paraded in character costume in a procession.

Miss Elizabeth Tebay, in the centre of the photograph, walks in the gala procession of 1913

At the front of the groups of children are Edith & Kath Danson. One of the sweeps was Tommy Roskell; his uncle provided the banner the children are carrying. They were captured by the camera about 1912.

Horses continued to be used in gala processions into the 1960s. The picture is particularly interesting as they are passing property in Church Street in the process of demolition and rebuilding on the site of the old Market Hall, itself demolished in the 1930s.

The Teanlowe provides a backdrop to preparations for a gala procession in the 1980s. It is usually held on the first Saturday in June.

The River Wyre was remarkable for its safe waters and could be entered in stormy weather, which would have been impossible in the Lune or the Ribble. However, until the first bridge was built it was not possible to take full advantage of its potential for commercial development, and it was reported that *'hourly inconvenience is felt by the inhabitants'*. A ferry between Skippool and Wardleys on the far side of the river ran with a wide flat bottomed boat in the 1600s or a wide-wheeled farm wagon when the water was too low for a boat.

Poulton had two ports, one on either bank of the River Wyre; on the south side at Skippool and on the north side at Wardleys in Hambleton. This was an important trading facility for Poulton during the 18th century. Skippool is now no more than a mooring. Ferries had existed at Aldwath, Wardleys and Knott End, but by the 1860s increased agricultural markets lead to the building of the Shard Toll Bridge, authorised by a private Act of Parliament. The bridge opened in 1864 and although a report in 1937 recommended a new crossing, it was not until 1992 that a new bridge, free from toll, replaced the original.

In 1938 there was a change in the method of collecting tolls on Shard Bridge - instead of dropping your penny in the hat, cap or outspread palm, a couple of men stand sentinel at the gate and in exchange for your toll give you a bridge ticket. After many years of increasing traffic across Shard Bridge with ensuing hold-ups as each motorist paid a toll on their way across in each direction, the new – free – bridge was welcomed by residents and visitors alike. The lower picture shows the new bridge under construction; it stands just a few yards from the site of the old one.

When William Gaulter took over as landlord of the Golden Ball in March 1850, he described his new venture as '*the leading commercial and posting house in the district*', with the house and stabling undergoing considerable alterations. It had '*well seasoned and steady horses, substantial conveyances and attentive ostlers and several new loose boxes for horses and a lock-up coach house*'. The hotel served home-brewed beer, choice wines and spirits and had well aired beds.

In 1895 The Bull was advertised as a family and commercial hotel with billiards and a bowling green, stabling and loose boxes. It had recently undergone extensive alterations and improvements. The Bull housed the excise office in 1851 when John Dagger was the landlord.

From the early 19th century Bull Street consisted of small properties, a lot of them owned by John Hodgson. John and his brother William had done well from their tanning business in Poulton and both had retired in their mid-forties. The cottages were occupied by tradesmen and women - shoemakers, clog and patten makers, seamstresses, agricultural and other labourers.

Pattens were a form of footwear which had become extinct by the mid-19th century. They were essentially an iron ring worn under a boot or shoe which raised the footwear out of the mud or puddles common before paved roads. The iron, later rubber, nailed to the sole of clogs removed the need for a separate piece of footwear.

As was often the case, local joiners doubled up as coffin makers and undertakers. James Dobson, a town councillor, gave his name to an avenue in Normoss, on the outskirts of Poulton Urban District Council's area.

Queen Victoria's Diamond Jubilee 1897. The programme of events closely mirrored those events of the Golden Jubilee in 1887. The procession began at 11am in the Market Place. Lead by a military band followed by the clergy, the main part of the procession was made up of school children from Staining, Carleton, Hardhorn and Poulton waving handkerchiefs and wearing their best clothes. The fire brigade, two more bands and representatives of local organisations completed the parade. In the afternoon all the children enjoyed games and the elderly – those over 50 years of age – were treated to a meal.

What is even more interesting than the celebrations is the record of demolition going on in the background. This site had previously been occupied by a couple of single-storey whitewashed cottages, but a more imposing building was later erected on the site before this too was demolished and the single-storey police station was built.

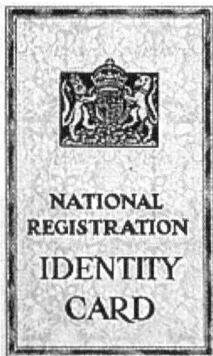

VE Day celebrations in First Avenue, Poulton - 1945.

King Edward VII died in 1910 and a memorial service was held in St Chad's. As was the custom on both sombre and joyous occasions, a procession was formed consisting of bands and civic dignitaries.

POULTON-LE-FYLDE
URBAN DISTRICT COUNCIL

CORONATION
of
HER MAJESTY
QUEEN ELIZABETH II

2nd June, 1953

Souvenir Programme

The old buildings on the east side of Church Street are in the process of being demolished. This occasion appears to have been in the year of the Coronation of King George V and Queen Mary in 1910. The demolition of the old buildings which backed onto St Chad's churchyard along Ball Street and Church Street was a scheme to commemorate Queen Victoria's Diamond Jubilee, in 1897. It took several years for the work to be completed.

One of the oldest buildings in the town centre was a five-bay three-storey building which can be seen in the distance in Church Street. This photograph dates from about 1915.

By the time of its demolition in the 1930s, this imposing building standing at the end of Church

Street was known as the Market Hall. In the period after its demolition several other buildings and businesses have occupied the site. Many of the buildings behind the Market Place were demolished during the late 1960s and early 1970s, in common with rebuilding which was taking place across the country at that time.

Photographs of the old buildings show how much the town was in need of regeneration. Unfortunately, with the destruction of the dangerous and unhealthy went much that would nowadays be valued for its history and character – the tithe barn, the market hall and a variety of small cottages which might have been worth restoring.

This aerial photograph was taken before many of the changes where brought about in the town centre. It shows clearly the amount of demolition which took place in order for the Teanlowe centre and the neighbouring car park to be built.

'Dudley Hall' in Bull Street, where the Library is now is. In 1891 John Swarbrick, famous for producing parched peas - soaked, roasted and sold from the house - lived here. Swarbrick is a long established Fylde name.

In 1892 *'the Institute'* was opened, with classes in dressmaking, cookery, laundry work, book keeping, shorthand and drawing. All classes were to be held in the Poulton Institute and students would be conveyed to the centre from the outlying districts. The classes were not a great success: 425 students enrolled of whom 30 failed to attend altogether and a *'large number'* only attended a few times.

The Lancashire & Cheshire Bee Keepers Association arranged for talks to be held at the Institute *'being valuable to the artisan living in the outskirts of towns and to the cottager and labourer. Where competent knowledge of bee keeping has been acquired a comparatively small outlay of money and spare time afford in good seasons a pecuniary reward equal to the keeping of a pig or sometimes even a cow'* .

The present library was one of the first buildings in the wave of development which took place in Poulton in the late 1960s and early 70s. The library has had many alterations to its interior design since it was opened in 1966, with its gallery reached by a spiral staircase.

65

In June 1916 William Hughes of Warbreck Drive and Mrs. Sarah Brown of Buchanan Street, Blackpool built the 'Rialto' cinema in Vicarage Road. Unfortunately the venture failed and they were declared

bankrupt the following year. In 1953, Queen Elizabeth was crowned and the nation watched the coronation ceremony for the first time on television; in Poulton it was possible to watch it at the Rialto cinema and in the Church Hall free of charge. The rate of growth in house building in Poulton in the 1950s was very rapid and in 1955 there was no Poulton Gala because land was no longer available as a gala field. Instead there was a children's treat with a film show at the Rialto, a meal and sports in the evening on Wednesday July 27th during the school holidays.

This is Ball Street showing the demolition of Charnley's garage. E.H. Booth's was to be built on the site. At the time there was no one-way system round the town centre with all roads carrying traffic in both directions. Day's butchers – the property on the left – was originally one of a pair of houses, which in the 1850s was a school run by Thomas Hammond. As well as day pupils, seventeen others boarded at the school, coming from as far afield as Scotland, Liverpool and Kendal. The school flourished until the 1880s. The original front entrance to one of the houses is still recognisable as such although it is now a shop entrance. The daughter of Thomas and Jane Hammond, Isabella Ellen, was to become the wife of Sir William Hodgson.

An aerial photograph taken from St Chad's church tower in the 1960s. The tithe barn has already been demolished as cars are parked on the site. The old houses on the other side of Tithebarn Street still stand though they too would soon go to be replaced by commercial property and the entrance to another car park. Notice that the street was still used by '*two-way*' traffic.

Singleton, listed in the Domesday Survey of 1086, was divided into *'Great Singleton'*, the main village, and *'Little Singleton'*, which lies on the road to Poulton. Singleton was a grange, or farm, belonging to Cockersand Abbey which passed to the Crown at the Dissolution. From that time it was owned by various local families. *'Bankfield'*, another large estate in Singleton, was owned for a long period by the Harrison family. Singleton windmill stood just outside the village on the road to Kirkham.

The main street in Singleton is known as *'The Village'*. The house on the left was the Post Office, one of at least three locations the Post Office has been in. There is still a Post Office in Station Road. Letters were hand stamped *'Great Singleton'* by the postmaster or postmistress. The photograph would have been taken standing in front of where today is Singleton Service Station, on the left.

Thomas Miller, a wealthy cotton manufacturer from Preston, built Singleton Hall in 1855 for himself and his large family. He also financed the building of St Anne's church in 1860 and the pub *The Miller Arms*. Singleton Hall remained in the family until 1946. In the grounds are two graves - one to a champion shirehorse and the other to the family's dogs. The hall was converted into apartments in 2006.

In 1882 Thomas Horrocks Miller designed the building that housed the village's fire engine. Today it houses an electricity substation. The road to the right of the fire station is called *The Village*, and to the left is Church Road.

A fire in Elswick caused damage to a terrace of thatched cottages. The fire crew from Singleton were available to deal with it. This was in the early years of the century and it is likely that the fire was out when the *emergency services* arrived.

THE SQUARE, STAINING VILLAGE.

Telephone 25703
V. & F. M. HALLAM
High-class Bakers
and Confectioners
Home-Made Bread & Pies
8 THE STRAND, STAINING ROAD END
HARDHORN

Staining is linked to farming. The windmill was built in the late 18th century, on the 55 feet above sea level contour, to grind locally-grown corn.

Staining had a monastic grange (a farm owned and run by a monastery) and it was probably based on what was to become Staining Hall, which was demolished in the 1980s to make way for the houses in King's Close. Farming is reflected in the pub's name, 'The Plough' which was in existence in the early 1800s. Here we see how close to the road the pub's front door was, before it was replaced in 1986 by the present building.

John Robert Wainman from Carleton was a joiner and blacksmith in Staining village in the early 1900s.

In 1902 he lived with his family at 'Thornfield House', now the 'office' for a small caravan site, and had his workshop a little further down towards the Plough, on the side opposite the school. His smithy site later became an egg-packing station and is now occupied by houses, one of which is called 'The Forge'.

70

STAINING ROAD.

E.3826.

Staining Road End. The Newton Arms Hotel was to be built on the field at the left of the picture in the 1956.

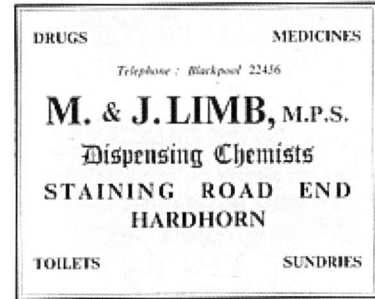

DRUGS   MEDICINES

Telephone : Blackpool 22456

M. & J. LIMB, M.P.S.

Dispensing Chemists

STAINING   ROAD   END
HARDHORN

TOILETS   SUNDRIES

The farmyard scene is from the 1930s. The Pearce family, shown in the centre of the photograph, farmed at Stanley House Farm, built in the 1880s. It ceased to be operational in the 1990s when second-generation Steve Earnshaw sold the house and its adjacent buildings as housing.   It had its own spring-fed well. The farm's name shows some connection with the Stanleys, Lord Derby's family, who owned much Fylde farmland. It may be that Miles Shaw, who built the house, had bought the land from the Derby estate.

Poulton District Council was formed in 1900 and ended when Poulton became part of Wyre Borough Council in 1974.

Our look at Poulton ends in the town centre. Ball Street - taking its name from the Golden Ball pub on the far right – as it was on a sunny summer day in the late 1950s. The Co-op has its blinds down against the sunshine, cars are parked on both sides of the street. Gordon Bentley was a newsagent and men's hairdressers. Other shops included Day's butchers, the Exclusive Ladies Hairdressers, Robinson's opticians and Abbott's shoe shop. Charnley's garage stood on the site of where today is Booth's supermarket.

The shield illustrates the history of Poulton through heraldic symbols. A ship sails on, flying the flag of St George, alluding to Poulton's former port at Skippool. The ship's sail is furled to illustrate that in modern times the ancient port has lost its former importance. The rose of Lancaster stands between two crosses – representing St Chad and the diocese of Lichfield, of which the ancient parish of Poulton was once a part. The whole is surmounted by the crest, which takes the form of the stocks and market cross. The motto translates as '*May we flourish beneath the Cross*', alluding to the importance of Poulton both as an ecclesiastical and commercial centre. The arms were designed by H Ellis Tomlinson, a master at Baines' Grammar School, in 1950.